GRAVE GOSSIP

YOU'RE NOT FORGOTTEN

By Sam Silver

Mr. Graves Headstone, Chicago IL

Printed by Lulu Press

HF0000.A0   A00   2016
299.010 00–dc22 2012989790

First Edition

ISBN: 978-1-387-97911-0

14 13 15 11 13 / 10 9 8 5 66 5 49 1 2 1

(Cover Eternal Silence, alternatively known as the Dexter Graves Monument or the Statue of Death, is a monument in Chicago's Graceland Cemetery. It is a bronze sculpture set on and back dropped by black granite. It was created by American sculptor Lorado Taft in 1909. According to folklore looking into the eyes of the statue will give the viewer a vision of their own death.)

Thank You Betty, Clarence, David, Ellen, Linda, Lulu, Mick and everyone who helped bring this book together.

CONTAINS

How did I get into cemetery history and lore? Easy, it is a quick and cheap place to stretch your legs on road trips. As a kid, it was simple to get the parents to stop at a passing graveyard so I could take a break from my annoying little brother. At first, that is all it was, and they were everywhere.

But then as I grew up, I started to get curious. Why would a cemetery need a clock tower? The dead cannot tell time, right? Why were some beautifully kept up and others abandoned? Why did some have guards with guns at the gate? I started to read up on histories and any other information on cemeteries I could get my hands on. A general search for any cemeteries began, however, my notes were not yet started, so some photos don't have descriptions. I also started searching for family graves, many of which were lost in the bushes, literally.

The family search led to my latest development in my searching, the headstones themselves. Why would there be a pyramid in the middle of the rural heart of America? Why were some small and broken while others looked like a little home? The details within the cemeteries just drew me in. A man with a headstone stating he had been struck by lightning fourteen times. A baker who had his tombstone shaped into a three-tier cake.

The idea for a book soon developed as a way to help organize my growing notes. Some items I found I never could describe. For example, the symbol "OWBI" in a semi-circle. Those items are not in this book. However, I have found many symbols, materials, and styles which are included within.

As another note, many photos are from the Midwest, where I live; however, I also included my travels including Colma, New

Orleans, Boston and more. And if you find your family within, no harm intended. Your family just made for a great example.

Dead men may not tell tales, but the symbols on their tombstones do. What religion were they? What club did they belong to? What was their occupation? All and more can be found on monuments. Don't be afraid, open the gate and come in.

A cemetery is where...lives are commemorated, deaths are recorded - families are reunited, memories are made tangible and love is undisguised. This is a cemetery.

In America, whenever an area has newly settled the need for burial soon followed. The deceased was usually buried near the place of death and often in an unmarked grave. America's earliest burial grounds were not attractive, tranquil places. Graves were not located in neat rows and maintenance was minimal.

Sometimes cemeteries were located on a piece of land that could not be used for farming. The grass was allowed to grow long, and animals grazed on the site. It was a useful place, a highly visible reminder to every one of the brevity of life and the uncertainty of the afterlife.

When settlements had progressed beyond the pioneer stage burials became more ritualized. The family burying ground, with its tall, flat, rectangular stones, was a familiar sight in rural areas, as was the churchyard or community cemetery in villages or township centers.

Often cemeteries that began as a family burying grounds later were deeded for use as community cemeteries. The evolution of styles can often be seen. Others, however, were initially platted as cemeteries and had an administrative body for the day-to-day management.

Increased urbanization and its accompanying population density caused problems with the air and water in large cities and resulted in epidemics of smallpox, cholera, diphtheria, and other life-threatening diseases. It was believed that cemeteries contributed to the contamination of the water supply. New graves were thus located on the outskirts of urban centers.

Most larger non-Catholic cemeteries established from the 1840s to the 1870s emulated Mt. Auburn in their picturesque planning and landscape. With the evolution of the designed cemetery the earlier term "burial ground" was replaced with "cemetery" from the Latin "to sleep."

In 1869 New York art critic Clarence Cook agreed with Andrew Jackson Downing, a horticulturist and author, in that cemeteries were "all the rage." They were "famous over the whole country, and thousands of people visited them annually."

Technological advances, among them the invention of the lawnmower, led to progressively simpler cemetery designs. The memorial park cemetery, which gained popularity in the mid to late twentieth century, forbade the use of upright gravestones, in favor of small flat markers embedded in the ground. These cemeteries were typically privately owned and well maintained.

In the twentieth century, cemeteries were designed by cemetery professionals rather than landscape architects and/or horticulturists. And a growing number of them are run like a corporate business where profit is counted.

So, you're dead - now what? Today, thankfully, it is nearly impossible to be buried alive accidentally or be threatened by grave robbers. If you died at a nursing home or hospital, you would automatically receive all the official paperwork needed to move on to the next steps. Your survivors will need this paperwork later. If you died at home, have your survivors call the local hospital or social service, and they can help them.

Now the funeral and burial start. You arranged everything ahead of time, right? Did you make out your advanced directive? You let them know your wishes and customs, all written down and ready to go. Many of us will end up in a cemetery somewhere. Some may be off to sea in a blaze of glory, or the local cliff to let the birds pick the bones clean, or to the local science lab or perhaps even under the roses out back - your body will go somewhere.

A tombstone tourist (otherwise known as a "cemetery enthusiast", "cemetery tourist", "grave hunter", "graver", or "taphophile") describes an individual who has a passion for and enjoyment of cemeteries, epitaphs, gravestone rubbing, photography, art, and history of (famous) deaths. Every cemetery has its own little story to tell.

I like visiting the cemetery (graveyard, burial ground, final resting place, garden, holy land, whatever and wherever...). They're not all spooky or creepy, many of them are quite beautiful. You can find art, history, relatives and more. There are too many cemeteries, too many beliefs, too many styles of burial, to fit into one book, but hopefully, this will guide you through some of the many options that are available.

Let's start your tour at the gate with some different forms. Some people are merely buried on or near the family property. This is one of the simplest and oldest burial forms. Many people are bringing this way back with a home preparation of the deceased and green burial.

But there are many places to go, and cemeteries come in a variety of styles. Many are traditional, but other methods depend on your religion or your region. If you were cremated or not cremated also determines the type you may be looking for. I have also included Pet Cemeteries below since many traditional sites don't allow pet burials. Below are some other examples:

Columbarium Wall

Columbarium walls are a standard feature of many cemeteries, reflecting the increasing use of cremation rather than burial. While cremated remains can be kept at home by families in urns or scattered in some significant or attractive place, neither of these approaches allows for a long-lasting commemorative plaque to honor the deceased nor provides a place for the more full circle of friends and family to come to mourn. Therefore, many cemeteries now offer walls (typically of brick or rendered brick construction) with a rectangular array of niches, with each slot being big enough to accommodate a person's cremated remains. Columbarium walls are a very space-efficient use of land in a cemetery compared with burials and a niche in a columbarium wall is a much cheaper alternative to a burial plot.

Dead Cemetery

Most sites die because they are abandoned. Some are left because the family has moved away or died off. No living family members or member of the community feel a personal connection to those who are buried there. Others are abandoned because of the age. The cemetery was once a commercial venture, but today it is full and lacking any perpetual care funds; there is no money to maintain the graves. The owner has just abandoned the property. No more burials occur at these sites.

Family Cemetery

While unusual today, family (or private) cemeteries were a matter of practicality during the settlement of America. If a municipal or religious cemetery had not been established, settlers would seek out a small plot of land, often in wooded areas bordering their fields, to begin a family plot. Sometimes, several families would arrange to bury their dead together. While some of these sites later grew into actual cemeteries, many were forgotten after a family moved away or died out.

Graveyard

A graveyard is any place set aside for long-term burial of the dead, with or without monuments such as headstones. In countries with a Christian tradition, it is usually located near and administered by a church. From the early 19th century, new burying grounds were frequently founded as cemeteries, which are burying grounds that are usually separate from a church or parish.

Mass Grave

A mass grave is a grave containing multiple numbers of human corpses, which may or may not be identified before burial. Mass graves are usually created after a large number of people die or are killed, and there is a desire to bury the corpses quickly for sanitation or legal concerns. In disasters, mass graves are used for infection and disease control. Many times with catastrophe, only a memorial marks the event if nobodies survive.

Showmen's Rest (shown above) in Forest Park, IL is a 750 plot section of Woodlawn Cemetery where a mass grave of 56 (or perhaps 61) employees of the Hagenbeck-Wallace Circus were interred.

Memorial Park

A lawn cemetery, or garden or park, is covered in grass. Each grave is marked with a commemorative plaque placed horizontally at the head of the grave at ground-level. While families usually are still involved in the design and information contained on the slab, generally the size and materials of the plaque are constrained by the cemetery authorities, who often strongly encourage (or in some cases mandate) the use of a standard design.

Monumental Cemetery

A monumental cemetery is the traditional style of a cemetery with mostly headstones or other monuments made of marble, granite or similar materials rise vertically above the ground. Monumental cemeteries are often regarded as unsightly due to the random collection of statues and headstones they contain. Also, as maintenance of the tombstones is the responsibility of family members, over time many gravestones are forgotten about and decay and become damaged. For cemetery authorities, monumental cemeteries are difficult to maintain.

National Cemetery

A National Cemetery is generally a military cemetery containing the graves of U.S. military personnel, veterans, and their spouses but not exclusively so. Some National Cemeteries include the graves of critical civilian leaders and other prominent national figures. There are also state veteran cemeteries. The best known National Cemetery in Arlington National Cemetery (photo above) in Virginia, outside of Washington, D.C.

Natural Cemetery

A natural cemetery or eco-cemetery or green cemetery is a new style of a graveyard and is an area set aside for natural burials (with or without coffins). Natural burials are motivated by a desire to be environmentally conscious with the body rapidly decomposing and becoming part of the natural environment without incurring the environmental cost of traditional burials. Only flat stone markers are allowed.

Pet Cemetery

A pet cemetery is a cemetery for animals. Pets and other animals to which people are emotionally attached are often ceremonially buried. Most families bury deceased pets on their own properties, typically in the yard. Pet cemeteries offer single and multiple plots options. A specially designed pet casket or vault may be used. In cremation, the remains can be saved in an urn, buried, or scattered. In a memorial cremation, several pets are cremated together. The resulting cremated remains are then spread on the cemetery grounds. In most cases, pet cemeteries will have a chapel, and there will be facilities to hold either a non-denominational Christian or, alternatively, a non-religious ceremony.

Potter's Field

A potter's field, or common grave, was an American term for a place for the burial of unknown or indigent people. The expression derives from the Bible, referring to a field used for the extraction of potter's clay, which was useless for agriculture but could be used as a burial site. Many times these graves are near hospitals, old medical facilities or old state homes.

Prison Cemetery

A prison cemetery is a cemetery reserved for prisoners. Generally, the remains of inmates who are not claimed by family or friends are interred in prison cemeteries and include convicts executed for capital crimes. All of the gravestones are simple; some contain names and dates, while the older stones simply contain a prisoner number.

Religious Cemetery

Religious cemeteries are usually affiliated with specific religious sects or congregations. They are privately owned spaces, and qualification for entry depends on the individual practices of the religion and its followers. Most common are Catholic and Jewish.

Sea Burial

Burial at sea is the disposal of human remains in the ocean, generally from a ship or boat. It is regularly performed by navies and is done by private citizens in many countries.

Traditional Cemetery

A cemetery is a spatially defined area where the remains of deceased people are buried or are otherwise interred. The term cemetery (meaning: sleeping place) implies that the land is specially designated as a burial ground. The intact or cremated remains of deceased people may be interred. The remains may be buried in a grave, commonly referred to as burial, or may be interred in a tomb, an above-ground crypt, a mausoleum, columbarium, or other edifices.

Ok, now we know where your remains are going, but what about a marker? If you were buried at home, it might just be a rock or tree. Alternatively, if you have a sea burial, perhaps a memorial plaque on land or no marker at all.

Headstones come in a wide range of forms and types. The style of burial from the last chapter may determine the kind of marker you can use. Your region may also play a large part if you live in a floodplain an above ground tomb is your only choice. I can't list them all so take a look at your local cemeteries for other local ideas. Below are some ideas to start your imagination:

Barrel-vaulted Tomb

A tomb characterized by a vaulted roof, usually constructed of brick and then plastered, and typically employing a facade variation. Construction of the vaulted ceiling of these tombs using block required a fair level of expertise as is amply illustrated by the masonry work of this era. The false lintel slab supplanted the use of the vaulted ceiling in the mid-nineteenth century.

Bi-columnar Headstone

A bi-columnar headstone, which is also called a Gateway headstone, is a headstone with two columns that connect to make an arch. They can be anywhere from 2 feet to 20 feet tall. It is commonly used for husband and wife graves.

Block Marker

Block markers are tall, broad, and thick, and usually, have rounded tops. They are about two feet high and two feet across. They are typically made of granite. They have been used in pioneer times, Victorian times, and are still used today. Block markers come in many different shapes and designs.

Box Tomb

Box tombs are built with a ceiling and walls but no floor. They appear to be a "box" on the ground; however, they are about five feet deep. They were built this way to fool grave robbers into thinking that the body was inside the box when they were deep inside the ground.

Chest Tomb

Chest tomb looks like a broad chest or trunk. The epitaph is almost always found on the top of the monument. Although it appears that the tomb could contain a body, most of the time they do not; the body is buried.

Coffin Tomb

A coffin is a box a funerary used in the display and containment of dead people – either for burial or cremation. Gravestones are shaped like a casket or coffin.

Column Headstone

A column is like an obelisk, except more pillar-like. Columns can be found on family burial sites or the graves of those with high social statuses. The columns can be Egyptian, Roman, or Greek in design.

Comb Grave

A stone structure built over an in-ground grave that is triangular in shape. It most often consists of two rectangular sandstone slabs placed together to form a gabled roof over the grave.

Compound Marker

A multiple element marker. An upright slab, embedded in an original separate masonry base. Or perhaps, an associated pair of vertical plates, usually of the same shape but different height embedded in an original separate masonry base, which defines the grave. Or, one or more base levels supporting any other combination of architectural or sculptural form. Maybe some other combination marker.

Coping Grave

An above ground burial. Uncovered empty chambers framed by stone, brick, and plaster. They are filled with earth and are built up to 3 feet from the ground. This allows for burial in the soil. They can repeatedly entomb in one coping.

Exedra

A large monument that is shaped

like a long, curved bench, but there are also many examples where the seat is straight. It is used as an element of landscape design and most also contain statues.

Family Plot

Some people order a small amount of land in a graveyard that will be set aside for their family. These areas are called family plots, and a low brick wall usually surrounds them. Today some cemeteries don't allow family plots, but they do let you choose where you are buried. Most plots vary from a few feet to a few yards across. The majority of family plots were bought while people were first coming to America. Some families even have their cemeteries.

General Headstone

Marker or Headstone is any non-tomb mortuary structure which marks a below-grade burial but does not contain an interment and whose form is often sculptural. It is usually an upright stone marker with a base; traditionally inscribed with demographic information, epitaphs, or both; sometimes decorated with a carved motif.

Gothic Headstone

Gothic headstones usually are about two feet tall, not very thick, and made of marble. They typically have a pointed arch at the top of them, and can sometimes have two arcs. They were popular from about 1850 to the early 1900s.

Ground Level Headstone

A ground level, or flush marker, the headstone is usually flat and less than an inch above the ground. Often, they do not have much information on them.

Ledger Stone

Ledgers are a large and flat stone that is placed on top of the grave site. It sits flush with the ground. They can be plain or inscribed. Some have headstones and footstones. Ledgers often contain detailed information about the deceased.

Mausoleum

A mausoleum is an external free-standing building constructed as a monument enclosing the interment space or burial chamber of a deceased person or persons - a large tomb. Some are private family based while others are public cemetery based. Usually stone building with places for the entombment of the above dead ground. A Christian mausoleum sometimes includes a chapel.

Mausoleum Baroque

Baroque architecture is a term used to describe the building style of the Baroque era, begun in late sixteenth century Italy, that took the Roman vocabulary of Renaissance architecture and used it in a new rhetorical and theatrical fashion, often to express the triumph of the Catholic Church and the absolutist state. Mausoleums have a flowing design with lots of decoration.

Mausoleum Classical

Classical architecture is architecture derived in part from the Greek and Roman architecture of classical antiquity, enriched by classicizing architectural practice in Europe since the Renaissance. Mausoleums contain columns; looking similar to structures built by the ancient Greeks.

Mausoleum Egyptian

The Nile valley has been the site of one of the most influential civilizations which developed a vast array of diverse structures encompassing ancient Egyptian architecture. The architectural monuments, which include the Great Pyramid of Giza and the Great Sphinx of Giza, are among the largest and most famous. Mausoleums that are shaped like pyramids, or tombs that contain sphinxes, a symbol of a circle with vulture wings, or twin cobras. Also, an obelisk is also a form of Egyptian architecture.

Mausoleum Gothic

Gothic architecture is a style of architecture that flourished during the high and late medieval period. Its characteristic features include the pointed arch, the ribbed vault, and the flying buttress. Mausoleums have lots of towers and pointed arches.

Obelisk

Obelisks are usually found on the graves of people with high social status or family burial sites. Obelisks typically have a square base, and a long middle piece called a shaft. They are shaped to look like a finger pointing to heaven or a ray from the sun. Obelisks were most popular during the Victorian era, and are very noticeable in cemeteries.

Obelisk, Cross Vault

A cross vault obelisk has a square base with tapers going upward. The top of the tombs looks like the top of a church or a house. The lines on the top look as if they would be touching. This is from the Victorian era and was common in the 1800s. They are usually found on people of high social status. They stand out and are quickly noticed.

Parapet Tomb

A single or multiple vault tomb possessing a raised parapet (a low wall surmounting the structure's exterior walls or at a roofs perimeter) front concealing the roof behind.

Pitched Roof Tomb

A basic tomb type in which the roof is pitched, and usually defined either by end gables or a facade variation. Facades are typically pedimented (triangular), truncated (a modified pediment in which the top is flat, and usually serves as the base of a vase, cross, or monument), or elevated with a center lunette. The pedimented version often contains acroteria on each end (a corner ornament). This style is found in multiple and society tombs.

Pulpit Headstone

Pulpit tombstones are also known as slant face and are usually made of granite or marble. They were commonly used from the 1880s to 1910, and even to 1930. Often they look like an open book or a small lectern. Sometimes they resemble a bible, and if the bible or book is opened near the beginning, the person died at an early age.

Pyramid

An outer pyramid surfaces are triangular and converge to a single point at the top. A variation of the stepped-tomb, in which instead of a flat or pitched roof, a pyramid form was used. Civilizations have built pyramids in many parts of the world.

Raised Top Tombstone

A raised top tombstone would be flat to the ground if it weren't for the raised top, as the name suggested. However, the raised top is not very elevated, only coming about six inches above the ground. The top is generally flat.

Rock Cairn

A cairn is a pile of loose rocks and stones, which tends to be erected over a single or multiple burial or cremation. It is a mound of stones built as a memorial or a marker.

Sarcophagus

In its classical form, this tomb style resembles an actual coffin covered with a massive stone lid, resting either on a podium or a low foundation. Large tombs that look like they would contain a body. However, most of the time the body is buried under them.

Scroll Tombstone

A scroll tombstone is a tombstone that looks like a scroll. The scroll can be a single scroll that sits on a block or stone. The manuscript can also be open sometimes. The inscriptions are usually on the part of the tombstone, not the scroll.

Society Tomb

A society tomb is not an individual tomb, but a multi-layered tomb wall that contains several burial vaults. These types of monuments are often used by social or community groups so that all members would have burial space. They are like mausoleums in most ways, except that most people in a society tomb are connected in some way.

Table Tomb

Large, flat stone that is supported by legs that resemble pillars (usually six). The top of the stone contains the epitaph.

Tablet Headstone

Tablet headstones are tall, wide and not very thick. The can be straight or curved or have a fancy design. They are usually made of marble, most of the time have a curved top, and are common in 1880-1890.

Tumulus

A tumulus is a mound of earth and stones raised over a grave or graves. Tumuli are also known as barrows, burial mounds, Hugelgrab or kurgans, and can be found throughout much of the world. Looks often like a mausoleum that is built into a hill.

Vault

A vault is a container that you put the

casket. Leo Haaste created the first one, thinking that graves would be better in concrete. He started making them in the 1880s. Vaults can also be built with stone, plastic, and cement. They hold only one to two caskets.

Vault Oven

Wall vault is commonly known as an "oven" vault because of its arched shape. These walls of tombs were meant to be used to house the dead of for an entire family line. Well after the funeral, the remains could be pushed to the back receptacle, to make room for the next deceased.

Vault Wall

They are above ground. They are made out of stone or cement. It is an enclosed grave. It is usually made for just one or two people. They could be rows high and long. Some vaults are very extravagant, with stained glass windows and marble. Others are small and plain.

Are you keeping notes? You have selected where to go and how to mark the site so far. The type of marker you choose may only be available in a specific material, but there are many different types of materials used to make markers.

Some only last a short time, others may last several generations. A stone headstone may last decades, only to be consumed by a nearby growing tree. Or a wooden cross may last a few years and rot away. Cost also becomes a factor here. A marble mausoleum is going to cost a lot more than a glass block. Again, taking a tour of the local graveyard can help pinpoint local materials that can be used. Below are some examples:

Bronze

Bronze is an alloy of copper and tin, sometimes with other elements thrown in as well, such as phosphorous, manganese, aluminum, and silicon. Perfect for a headstone. To manufacture a bronze headstone, bronze is burnt at upwards of 1742 degrees, melted, and waxed together, hardened into a substantial very difficult to break, and capable plaque.

Concrete

Used in early cemeteries mainly to

create the plot surrounds especially in more steeply sloped plots and to form a strong foundation. It is gray or white unless artificially colored. Concrete was often seen used in conjunction with other materials. An excellent example of the use of concrete is the intricately shaped "tree stump" markers. Concrete's ability to be molded simplified the process compared to the much more labor-intensive method of carving limestone. The molding could be very detailed, including the bark and some limbs. Once a master form had been created, the marker could be reproduced in concrete with a minimum of additional effort.

Fieldstone

The earliest markers for graves were natural fieldstone, some unmarked and others decorated or incised using a metal awl. Typical motifs for the carving included a symbol and the deceased's name and age. Fieldstone grave markers were very common in early rural areas. Unfortunately, many fieldstone markers have been destroyed.

Glass

Favorite for years in Europe and America, stylish glass headstones and plaques offer an alternative to the traditional granite range while introducing an appropriately reflective quality to rural and metropolitan cemeteries and memorial parks. Glass in a more modern material but is longest lasting and can come in a wide variety of colors.

Granite

Granite is one of the most common and traditional materials for gravestone construction. It is a hard stone and requires skill to carve by hand. Modern methods of carving include using computer-controlled rotary bits and sandblasting over a rubber stencil. Leaving the letters, numbers, and emblems exposed on the stone, the blaster can create virtually any kind of artwork or epitaph. The color of granite is typically either gray or pink, with different grains, a mottled look, and shades available.

Homemade

Inexpensive homemade markers are sometimes seen in smaller and/or older grounds such as family graves or roadside markers. Some are made of wire, wood, brick, shells, plastic, concrete, a mixture or other materials on hand.

Iron

Iron grave markers and decorations were popular during the Victorian era, often being produced by specialist foundries or the local blacksmith. Iron, in various forms, was most commonly used for cemetery markers from about the 1830s to the early 1900s. Cast iron headstones have lasted for generations while wrought ironwork often only survives in a rusted or eroded state. What more commonly survive today are the beautiful cast iron metal fences that surround a grave.

Many cemeteries also contain small iron medallions placed beside the gravestone, which indicates the deceased's affiliation with fraternal or military associations.

Limestone

Both limestone and marble take carving well. Portland stone was a type of limestone commonly used in England - after weathering, fossiliferous deposits tend to appear on the surface. Limestone is calcite and ranges from pure white to brown. One of the best-known structures made of limestone are the pyramids. Some limestone is inclined to break away or come away in large flakes. Inscriptions are becoming hard to read or lost, and decorations are slowly vanishing.

Marble

Both limestone and marble take carving well. Marble is a recrystallized form of limestone. The mild acid in rainwater can slowly dissolve marble and limestone over time, which can make inscriptions unreadable. Marble became famous from the early 19th century, though it's extra cost limited its appeal. Marble may become discolored or soiled over time, and its color may change from white to shades of gray through soiling. The stone also has a tendency to become increasingly yellow with time.

Plantings

Trees or shrubs, particularly roses, may be planted to mark the location of ashes. This may be accompanied by a small inscribed metal or wooden marker, popular in green cemeteries.

Pottery

Grave markers made of clay that has been hardened by heat. Pottery markers are generally of two types: earthenware, which is often unglazed and fired at a low temperature, and stoneware, which is glazed and fired at a high temperature.

Sandstone

Sandstone is durable, yet soft enough to carve easily. Some sandstone markers are so well preserved that individual chisel marks are discernible, while others have delaminated and crumbled to dust. Delamination occurs when moisture gets between the layers of the sandstone. As it freezes and expands the layers flake off. In the 17th century, sandstone replaced field stones in Colonial America. Sandstones were used from about 1650-1890. Sandstone is typically buff, gray, brown, red, purple, or pink in color.

Slate

Slate can have a pleasing texture but is slightly porous and prone to delamination. It takes lettering well, often highlighted with white paint or gilding. Slate is a hard yet brittle material typically dark blue, gray or black in color.

Wood

This was a favorite material during the Georgian and Victorian era, and almost certainly before, in Great Britain and elsewhere. Some could be very ornate, although few survive beyond 50–100 years due to natural decomposition. Wooden markers are still today used as a temporary grave marker until something more substantial can be organized as a permanent replacement.

Zinc

Zinc or White Bronze is actually sand cast zinc but called white bronze for marketing purposes. Zinc is a bluish-gray nonmagnetic, metallic element that is generally brittle but can be worked when heated. Almost all, if not all, zinc grave markers were made between 1874 and 1914. They are in cemeteries of the period all across the U.S. and Canada. They were sold as more durable than marble, about 1/3 less expensive and progressive. Customers could pick from a variety of panel designs, which were cast, and then bolted together. The handy thing about these was that panels could easily be replaced so that more names could be easily added to the monument. These markers are affectionately known as "zinkers."

So, now you know where your remains are going, and you know how you are going to mark the site but what are you going to put on your headstone? Many graves are labeled as a memorial to you, so you are not forgotten.

The symbols on the marker can tell a lot about who you were. There are millions of symbols, some universal and others more personal. If you are going to a Government National Cemetery or Memorial Park, your choice is more limited due to strict rules but for the most part, let your creativity flow. Below is only a small collection of examples:

A.O.U.W.
Ancient Order of United Workmen, a fraternal benefit society. The Ancient Order of United Workmen was a fraternal organization in the United States and Canada, providing mutual social and financial support after the US Civil War. It was the beginning of the American network of fraternal benefit societies.

A.R.
Arbeiter Ring, an American Jewish fraternal organization

committed to social justice. Later became the Workmen's Circle.

Alpha and Omega

First and last letters of the Greek alphabet. Symbolizes the beginning and the end. They are often found combined into a single symbol representing Christ.

American Legion

Found on graves of people who were American Legion members, an organization for veterans.

Anchor

Hope or eternal life. Early Christians used the anchor as a disguised cross, and as a marker to guide the way to secret meeting places. It can represent the Christian cross. A Christian symbol of hope, it is found as funerary symbolism in the art of the catacombs. Often on sailors' graves when setting amongst rocks. It can also be an official symbol in sea-faring areas or the attribute of Saint Nicholas, patron saint of seamen, symbolized hope and steadfastness.

An anchor with a broken chain stands for the cessation of life. Anchors are also a Masonic symbol for well-grounded hope; therefore they are often found on Masons' graves.

Angel

Guardian or messenger between God and man. Symbol of resurrection. A guide to heaven. An angel with open wings is thought to represent the flight of the soul to heaven. Angels may also be shown carrying the deceased in their arms as if taking or escorting them to heaven. Saint Matthew, one of the four evangelists, was often represented as a winged man.

Angel Black   (Oakland Cemetery in Iowa City)

The 9-foot tall statue was initially white but turned black shortly after being erected. Legend says that it becomes a shade darker every Halloween. Also, it is noted that the statue will kill anyone who touches it, except for virgins. People who have tried to deface the statue came down with strange ailments, which eventually killed them.

Angel Gabriel

Angel Gabriel with her horn.   An angel with a trumpet represents the Archangel Gabriel who stands ready to issue the call to resurrection. Or an angel blowing a trumpet may depict the day of judgment.

Angel Michael

Angel Michael by his sword. Only the Archangel Michael is clothed in armor. The sword He carries represents a cross but also a weapon in his war against the devil's warriors.

Angel Moroni

The angel was the guardian of the golden plates, which Latter Day Saints believe were the source material for the Book of Mormon.

Angel of Grief *(Cypress Lawn Cemetery in Colma)*

This style of a monument is also referred to as "Weeping Angel." Sorrow. A weeping angel symbolizes grief, especially mourning an untimely death.

Anvil

Martyrdom. Symbolizes the creation or forging of the universe. Also found on blacksmiths' graves.

Arch
The victory of life or success in death. The passage to heaven.

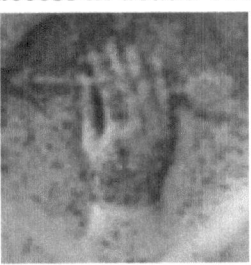

Arrow
Denotes mortality. Arrows symbolize death and martyrdom.

Artillery
Artillery, such as cannons, on a gravestone usually represents military service.

Atheist
Available emblem of belief for placement on government headstones and markers.

B.P.O.E.

B.P.O.E. stands for Benevolent Protective Order of Elks, a fraternal organization. The Elks are one of the largest and most active fraternal organizations in the United States, with over one million members. Their emblem often incorporates a clock tolling the eleventh hour, directly behind the representation of the elk head to represent the "Eleven O'Clock Toast" ceremony conducted at every BPOE meeting and social function.

B.R.T

Brotherhood of Railroad Trainmen. A fraternal organization for men who worked as trainmen.

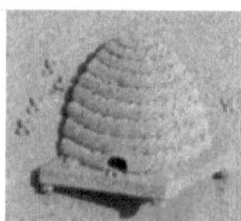

Beehive

Often used by the Freemasons and Independent Order of Odd Fellows. It symbolizes human industry, faith, education, and domestic virtues.

Bell

Often symbolizes a church bell, and therefore religion. Call to worship.

Bird

Peace, a messenger of God. Bird flying means Resurrection. These are symbolic of the "winged soul." The representation of the soul by a bird goes back to ancient Egypt. Some older burial art features only wings to convey the symbol of divine mission. Often denote the graves of children, eternal life.

Bird, Dove

The most common birds found on gravestones are doves. In Christian symbolism, it typically represents the Holy Ghost. Seen in both Christian and Jewish cemeteries, the dove is a symbol of resurrection, innocence, and peace.

An ascending dove represents the transport of the departed's soul to heaven. A dove descending represents a descent from heaven, assurance of safe passage. A dove lying dead symbolizes a life cut prematurely short. If the dove is holding an olive branch, it signifies that the soul has reached spiritual peace in heaven and refers to the dove Noah sent out to find land.

Bird, Eagle

Suggests courage and possibly a military career. Eagles are often seen on gravestones of Civil War veterans and indicate courage.   Saint John, one of the four evangelists, was often represented as an eagle.

Bird, Eagle, Double-headed

A Masonic symbol, part of the Scottish Rite. This one symbolizes the 32nd degree in this Rite.

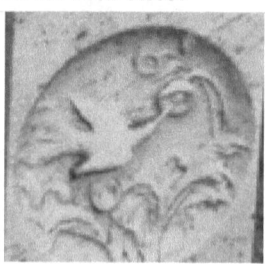

Bird, Hummingbird
Often found on infants' gravestones.

Bird, Owl

Wisdom, watchfulness. In Western culture, the owl is a symbol of knowledge, which dates back to Ancient Greece where the owl was the symbol of the goddess of wisdom, Athena.

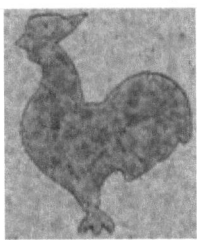

Bird, Rooster

Symbolizes an awakening, or calling attention to the person's death. It also signifies vigilance and the Resurrection.

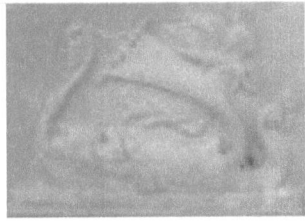

Boat or Ship

A voyage; crossing over to the other side. Could also be a boat builder or a sailor.

Bones

Death, decay, mortality. A reminder that death comes to everyone as indicated by the words 'Momento Mori,' meaning "Remember that you must die."

Book or Bible

Often used on the gravestones of ministers or clergymen. If a member of the clergy, sometimes the final sermon is written on the open pages.

However, it is sometimes found on gravestones of very devoted religious people also. A book on a tombstone may also depict learning, a scholar, a prayer, memory, or someone who worked as a writer, bookseller, or publisher. Books and scrolls can also represent the Evangelists. The open book describes the book of life. The closed book represents the end of earthly life, a completed life. A stack of Books are scholarly, educated.

MATT RIZZO - SCORTO

AUG. 13, 1913 — AUG. 23, 1987

Braille

The Braille system is a method that is widely used by blind people to read and write. Each Braille character or cell is made up of six dot positions, arranged in a rectangle containing two columns of three dots each.

Butterfly

Symbolizes resurrection, and also the soul leaving the body/flesh. The meaning is derived from the three stages of the life of the butterfly—the caterpillar, the chrysalis, and the butterfly. The three phases are symbols of life, death, and resurrection. It may also represent the heart and may be found on children's headstones.

Canadian Legion of British Empire Service League

A Canadian organization formed in the 1920's for war veterans and their dependents. Usually seen with a maple leaf.

Candle

Candle, with a flame – life. Candle being snuffed - mortality.

Chain

Medieval thinkers sometimes held that a golden chain bound the soul to the body. Broken links on a headstone can mean the severance and subsequent release of the spirit from the body. Chains are also the insignia of the International Order of Odd Fellows, so called because of their dedication to giving the indigent decent burials.

Child Sleeping

A sleeping child is a Victorian symbol for death. Figures of sleeping babies or children often appear with very few clothes, symbolizing that innocent young child had nothing to cover up or hide.

Church of World Messianity

Available emblem of belief for placement on government headstones and markers.

Circle

Eternity or Earth. The circle is pre-Christian, and its original symbolic meaning has been adopted by Christianity. It is universally known as the symbol of eternity and never-ending existence. Extremely common on grave sites, its general representation is a cross surrounded by a circle. Two circles, one above the other, represent earth and sky. Three interconnected circles represent the Holy Trinity.

Clock

Mortality, death or the passage of time. Represents the transitory nature of human existence. In psychoanalysis, it signifies human emotions. It also can denote new beginnings and opportunities. Sometimes it is set to the time of death.

Coffin

Symbolizes mortality and death.

Colonial Daughters

An organization for women who descended from an ancestor who rendered service in the Colonial Wars from 1607 to 1699.

Column

Mortality. A draped or broken column represents the break-in earthly to heavenly life. A broken column indicates a life cut short, a memorial to the death of someone who died young or in the prime of life, before reaching old age. Some columns you encounter in the cemetery may be broken due to damage or vandalism, but many columns are intentionally carved in the broken form. The draped arch also symbolizes mourning.

Community of Christ

Available emblem of belief for placement on government headstones and markers.

Compass and Square

Usually, have the letter "G" in the middle. The square and compass represent the transition from the material to the intellectual to the spiritual. Found on gravestones belonging to members of the Freemasons (Masons).

Cornucopia

Known as the "Horn of Plenty." Symbolizes an abundant, fruitful life. Also a symbol of the harvest, which in turn signifies the end of life.

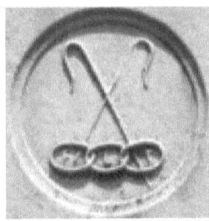

Crooks

Shepherds crooks, usually found on graves of Independent Order of Odd Fellows members (a fraternal organization). Symbolizes the opening of the earth to the heavens.

Cross and Crown

Symbolizes both victory and Christianity. Also, this symbol sometimes denotes a member of the York Rite Masons and symbolizes authority. Also available emblem of belief for placement on government headstones and markers.

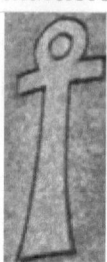

Cross Ankh

Also known as the Egyptian Cross, the Key of the Nile, the Looped Tau Cross, or the Ansate Cross. It was an Ancient Egyptian symbol of life and fertility, pre-dating the modern cross. The Coptic Christians used it as a symbol of life after death. The ankh has been used in magic, and today it usually symbolizes peace and truth.

Cross Celtic

The Celtic or Irish cross, taking the form of a cross within a circle, generally represents eternity. In Ireland, it is a popular legend that the Celtic Christian cross was introduced by Saint Patrick. Since its revival in the 1850s, the Celtic cross has been used extensively as grave markers. Also available emblem of belief for placement on government headstones and markers.

Cross Christian

Also known as the Latin cross. In early times, it was called god's mark. It is the most common symbol of Christianity, intended to represent the death of Jesus when he was crucified on the True Cross and his resurrection in the New Testament. Additionally available emblem of belief for placement on government headstones and markers.

Cross Episcopal

Available emblem of belief for placement on government headstones and markers. Essentially a Latin cross, with a circle enclosing the intersection of the upright and crossbar, as in the standing High crosses.

Cross Greek

Used mainly by Eastern Orthodoxy and Early Christianity Also known as the crux immissa quadrata. Has all arms of equal length and not much longer than the width. The same length drawings of the cross are pre-Christian, and in paganism, represented the four elements - earth, air, fire, and water. Also available emblem of belief for placement on government headstones and markers.

Cross Lutheran

Available emblem of belief for placement on government headstones and markers. The heart like shield is the symbol of the Holy Trinity.

Cross of Sacrifice or War Cross

A Latin cross with a superimposed sword, blade down. It is a symbol used by the Commonwealth War Graves Commission at the site of many war memorials. There is a Cross of Sacrifice located in Arlington National Cemetery by the graves of United States citizens who enlisted in the Canadian military and lost their lives during the First World War.

Cross Patriarchal

Similar to the simple Latin cross, the Patriarchal cross

possesses a smaller crossbar placed above the main one, so that both crossbars are near the top.

Sometimes the patriarchal cross has a short, slanted crosspiece near its foot. This slanted, lower crosspiece often appears in Byzantine Greek and Eastern European, as well as Eastern Orthodox churches. They have three bars that symbolize the cross Christ was crucified on.

The Russian Orthodox cross can be considered a modified version of the Patriarchal cross, having two smaller crossbeams, one at the top and one near the bottom, in addition to the longer crossbeam.

Cross Presbyterian
Available emblem of belief for placement on government headstones and markers. The Presbyterian Cross is often adorned with the symbol of a burning bush.

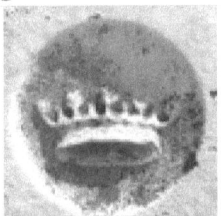

Crown
Victory or triumph over death. May be shown being offered to those on earth by angels.

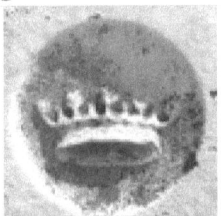

The degree of Pocahontas (sometimes seen as the Daughters of Pocahontas), organized in 1885 - the female auxiliary for the Improved Order of Redmen, a patriotic organization.

D.A.R.

Daughters of the American Revolution, a non-profit women's organization for the descendants of American Revolutionary War veterans.

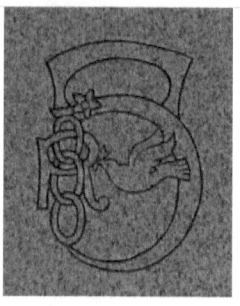

D.R.

Daughters of Rebekah. The branch was named after the Rebekah from the Bible whose unselfishness at the well represents the virtues of the society. The typical symbol for this female auxiliary of the Independent Order of Odd Fellows includes a half moon for "the value of regularity in work," a dove for peace, a lily for purity, and the intertwined letters D and R.

Other symbols commonly associated with the Daughters of Rebekah include the beehive, the moon (sometimes embellished with seven stars), the dove and the white lily. Collectively, these symbols represent the feminine virtues of industriousness at home, order and the laws of nature, and innocence, gentleness, and purity.

Dog

Loyalty, fidelity, watchfulness, and vigilance. Can be found in both human and pet cemeteries and may be a replica of the real-life dog.

Door

Door or Doors heavenly entrance. Passing through the door into a new state of being.

Dragon

A dragon is a legendary creature, typically with serpentine or reptilian traits, that feature in the myths of many cultures. There are two distinct cultural traditions of dragons: the European dragon, derived from European folk traditions and ultimately related to Greek and Middle Eastern mythologies, and the Chinese dragon, with counterparts in Japan, Korea, and other East Asian countries.

In Western folklore, dragons are usually portrayed as evil, with the exceptions mainly in Welsh folklore and modern fiction.

Chinese dragons traditionally symbolize potent and auspicious powers, particularly control over water, rainfall, hurricane, and floods. The dragon is also a symbol of power, strength, and good luck.

Drape

Mourning. The closing off of life, sometimes early. Refer to the veil between heaven and earth. Sometimes associated with an urn.

Elephant (Mass grave in Chicago)

Elephants are the largest living land animals on Earth today. Elephants are a symbol of wisdom in Asian cultures and are famed for their memory and intelligence. The elephant is also commonly seen as symbols for circus people.

Eucharist

The body and blood of Christ. Usually found on graves of

priests and nuns.

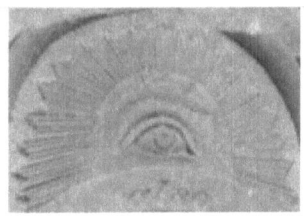

Eye

Usually found in a triangle or within a sunburst. This is a masonic symbol.

F of A

Foresters of America, a fraternal society founded in 1895 that provided life and disability insurance to its members. Usually contains an eagle, crossed flags, and a deer. Their motto was Liberty, Unity, Benevolence, and Concord.

F.A.T.A.L.

A motto of the Order of the Eastern Star stands for "Fairest Among Thousands, Altogether Lovely." Order of the Eastern Star, the largest fraternal organization in the world to which both women and men may belong. A woman must be related by birth or marriage to a Mason to become a member of OES, and a man must be a Mason to join.

F.C.B.

Symbol of the Knights of Pythias, a fraternal organization for government clerks. FCB means Friendship, Charity, and Benevolence. You may also see the skull and crossbones within a heraldic shield, a knight's helmet or the letters KP or K of P (Knights of Pythias) or IOKP (Independent Order of Knights of Pythias).

F.C.L.

The motto of the Women's Relief Corp. stands for "Fraternity, Charity, and Loyalty." The Woman's Relief Corps (WRC) is the official women's auxiliary to the Grand Army of the Republic, recognized in 1883.

F.F.C.

Symbol of the Improved Order of Red Men, a patriotic society. Their motto is Freedom, Friendship, and Charity.

F.L.T.

A symbol of the Independent Order of Odd Fellows (IOOF), a fraternal organization. Stands for Friendship, Love, and Truth.

F.O.E.

Symbol of the Fraternal Order of Eagles, a fraternal organization.

Father Time

A man with an hourglass and sickle. Death as the "last harvest." An old man with a beard, holding an hourglass and/or sickle.

Fish

Symbolizes Christianity. Also found with fisherman. Often

associated with Christ, with early Christian imagery and part of its coded language, it also indicates bounty or plentifulness.

Flag American

The American flag, a symbol of courage and pride, is generally found marking the grave of a military veteran in American cemeteries.

Flame or Torch

Eternity. An upside down torch represents the end of life. A lit or upright torch represents life.

Fleur-de-lis

In French, fleur de lis literally means "lily flower," it is used as a decorative design or symbol. While the fleur-de-lis has appeared on countless European coats of arms and flags over the centuries, it is mainly associated with the French monarchy in a historical context.

Freemasons

Freemasonry or Masonry consists of fraternal organizations that trace their origins to the local fraternities of stonemasons, which from the end of the fourteenth century regulated the qualifications of stonemasons and their interaction with authorities and clients.

The most common of the Masonic symbols is the compass and square standing for faith and reason. The letter G usually found in the center of the square and compass is said to represent "geometry" or "God."

G.A.R.

Grand Army of the Republic. A fraternal organization for men who fought and were honorably discharged from the Union Army, Navy, Marine Corps or Revenue Cutter Service during the Civil War.

Gate

A passage from earth to heaven. There are many different variations, usually with many symbolic motifs such as the sun, hand of God, dove and olive branch, diving dove, and others.

Geb
German for Geboren (born)

Gest
German for Gestorben (death)

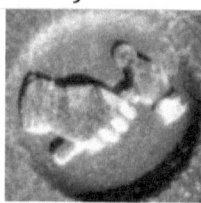

Hammer

A hammer symbolizes the power of creation. It can also represent the person's profession, such as a smith.

Hammer and Sickle
Emblem of the Communist movement, symbolizing the alliance of workers and peasants.

Hand Holding Heart
The hand holding a heart is a symbol used by the I.O.O.F

(Independent Order of Odd Fellows) and Masons, both fraternal organizations. It symbolizes charity.

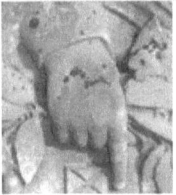

Hand Pointing Down
A hand with forefinger pointing down represents God reaching down for the soul.

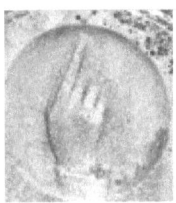

Hand Pointing Up
A hand with index finger pointing upward symbolizes the hope of heaven.

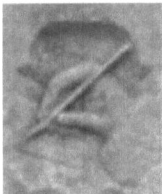

Hand Writing
Writing names in the book of life. Can also be found on writers' graves.

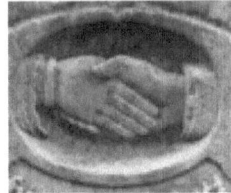

Hands Clasped
Farewell to earthly existence. Also unity or bond of marriage. Often used as a Masonic and I.O.O.F. symbol. The Native American culture use clasped hands to represent a Delaware Tribe grave.

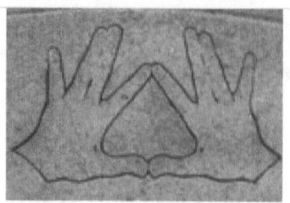

Hands Kohen or Cohanim

Hands with thumbs (and sometimes forefingers) joined. This is a Jewish symbol that represents members of the priestly tribe of Aaron. Also available emblem of belief for placement on government headstones and markers.

Hands Praying

Pious devotion. Asking God for eternal life.

Hands Reaching

Usually, the hand of God reaching down from the heavens, and the hand of the deceased reaching up to grab it in greeting.

Harp

A harp symbolizes praise to God. They are often carved with a broken string, representing a break in mortal life.

Heart

Person's spirit or soul. The heart is a symbol of life, love or immortality. Sometimes the sacred heart of Christ.

Hebrew Letters

Hebrew words for "Here Lies."

Horse

Death. White horses represent good, while black horses represent evil. An attribute of St. George, St. Martin, St. Maurice and St. Victor, all of whom are described in Christian art on horseback.

Horse with Soldier

A soldier's grave. If the horse has both front legs in the air, the person probably died in battle. If only one leg is raised, the person probably died as a result of wounds. And if the horse has all four legs on the ground, the person probably died of natural causes.

Horseshoe

The horseshoe can symbolize protection from evil, but may also signify an individual whose profession or passion involved horses.

Hourglass

Passage of time. Represents the impermanence of life; time has run out.

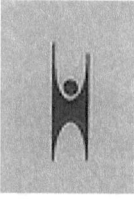

Humanist

Available emblem of belief for placement on government headstones and markers.

I.H.S.

Sometimes looks like a dollar sign. IHS stands for the first three letters of Jesus' name in the Greek alphabet. This symbol also stands for "in hoc signo," Latin for "by this sign we conquer," referring to the cross and means immortality.

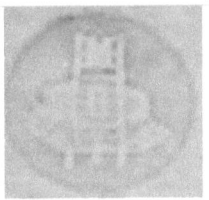

I.O.M.
Independent Order of Mechanics, a fraternal organization formed in 1868. Their symbols include Jacob's Ladder and an ark.

I.O.O.F.
International Order of Odd Fellows (IOOF). The key symbol for the IOOF is the three-link chain. It typically stands alone but can be seen with other symbols, including the letters FTL for Friendship, Love, and Truth.

In Memorium
"In memory of..." Common Latin phrase used on markers.

Islam (Crescent and Star)

A crescent moon and star symbol like the one pictured here is also a symbol of Muslim.

Jaycees

A non-profit organization for people between the ages of 18 and 41 that provides the tools they need to build the bridges of success for themselves in the areas of business development, management skills, individual training, community service, and international connections.

Jewish Menorah

A menorah, which is a candelabra with seven branches, is a Jewish symbol. It usually marks the grave of a righteous woman.

Judaism Star of David

Divine Protection. Available emblem of belief for placement on government headstones and markers.

K of C
Knights of Columbus, a fraternal organization for Catholic men.

K.O.T.M.
Symbol of the Knights of the Maccabees, a fraternal organization.

Knot
A tied knot symbolizes marriage and unity. The interlaced Celtic knot represents resurrection and life everlasting.

L.A. to B.R.T.
Symbol of the Ladies Auxiliary to the Brotherhood of Railroad Trainmen.

Lamb

Lambs are often seen on children's gravestones. A lamb represents innocence.

Lamb, Agnus Dei

Represents the Lamb of God. In Christian teachings, the Lamb of God refers to Jesus Christ in his role as the perfect sacrificial offering.

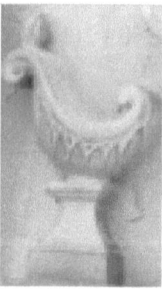

Lamp

Wisdom, faithfulness, knowledge, a love of learning, and the immortality of the Spirit.

Lion
The lion serves as a guardian in the cemetery, protecting a tomb from unwanted visitors and evil spirits. They also represent the courage, power, and strength of the deceased individual. Like other guardians, the lion's watch is as eternal as the stone of which it is depicted.

Lion Winged
Represents Saint Mark, one of the four evangelists.

Lion, Chinese
Chinese guardian lions, also known as stone lions in Chinese art and often called "Foo Dogs" in the West, are a standard representation of the lion in pre-modern China. They are believed to have mighty mythic protective powers that have traditionally

stood in front of Chinese Imperial palaces, Imperial tombs, government offices, temples, and the homes of government officials and the wealthy.

Lyre

A bridge between heaven and earth. Sometimes it has broken strings, symbolizing the end of life. Lyres are usually found on the graves of musicians.

M.W.A.

MWA stands for Modern Woodmen of America. This was the original name for the Woodmen of the World organization (WOW), an insurance company and fraternal organization. It is highly represented in cemeteries because, until the 1920s, one of the benefits of membership was a tombstone. Several organizations broke off from WOW including Women for Woodcraft, Neighbors of Woodcraft, Modern Woodmen of America, Woodmen Circle, and others.

Methodist
Available emblem of belief for placement on government headstones and markers. The cross and flame is the official symbol of the United Methodist Church since 1968.

Moon
The Moon has always been associated with magic, folklore, superstitious beliefs and ancient rituals. A common one found on graves is the rebirth. Many pagan and native traditions also involve the moon and its many cycles.

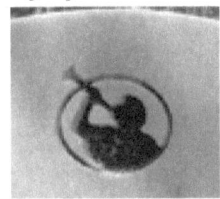

Mormon
The Church of Jesus Christ of Latter-day Saints. Available emblem of belief for placement on government headstones and markers.

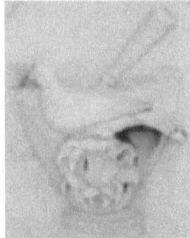

Mortar and Pestle
Usually found on the gravestones of pharmacists, and sometimes doctors.

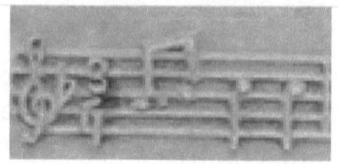

Music

Usually found on the graves of musicians. The music can be from a song the musician wrote, or it could be the deceased person's favorite hymn.

Nee

French for Born with Name (indicates a woman's maiden name, or a person's surname at birth).

Neighbors of Woodcraft

Seen on the gravestones of Neighbors of Woodcraft, a branch of Woodmen of the World (WOW). It is highly represented in cemeteries because, until the 1920s, one of the benefits of membership was a tombstone. Several organizations broke off from WOW including Women for Woodcraft, Neighbors of Woodcraft, Modern Woodmen of America, Woodmen Circle, and others.

O.E.S.

Order of the Eastern Star, the largest fraternal organization in the world to which both women and men may belong. A woman must be related by birth or marriage to a Mason to become a member of OES, and a man must be a Mason to join. The letters FATAL are also standard and refer to a portion of the Eastern Star oath.

O.S.C.
Order of Scottish Clans. A fraternal and benevolent society that was founded in 1878. They provided life and disability insurance to Scottish immigrants and their descendants. They became a part of the Independent Order of Foresters in 1971.

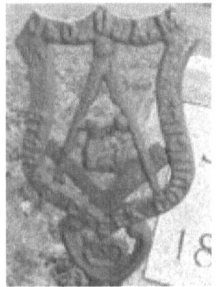

O.U.A.M. Jr.
The Junior Order of United American Mechanics. It is the oldest fraternal order that is still active in the United States. It was founded in Philadelphia, Pennsylvania in 1853.

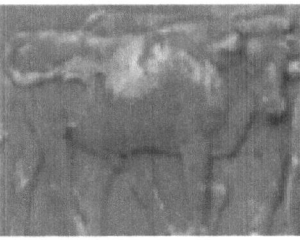

Ox
Patience, strength. The Celts valued Oxen for their virility and enduring physical productivity.

Ox Winged
Represents Saint Luke, one of the four evangelists.

P of H
Patrons of Husbandry, also known as the National Grange, an agricultural organization.

P.A.P.
Loyal Order of Moose (LOOM), a fraternal organization. P.A.P. stands for their motto: Purity, Aid, and Progress.

P.L.E.F.

Sometimes with crown and shield. Symbol of the Pythian Sisters, a fraternal organization for women. The letters PLEF stand for their motto: Purity, Love, Equality, and Fidelity.

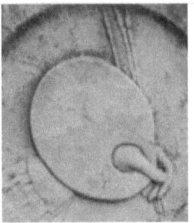

Palette and Brushes
Usually found on artists' gravestones.

Pebbles or Coins (on headstone)
The Jewish tradition of leaving a pebble or stone on top of a tombstone signifies that someone has honored the deceased person's memory with a visit to the grave.

In military cemeteries, sometimes coins are used to pay respect. A nickel indicates that you and the deceased trained at boot camp together, while a dime means you served with him in some capacity. By leaving a quarter at the grave, you are telling the family that you were with the soldier when he was killed.

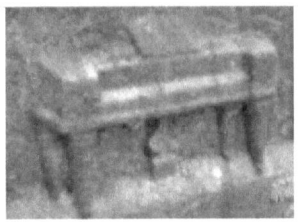

Piano
Usually found on the graves of musicians.

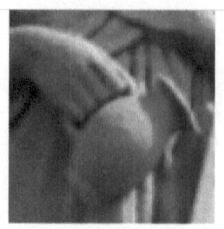

Pitcher

Often found on graves of prohibitionists. Represents virtue and control. If it is seen on a Jewish burial, it symbolizes a Levite, a person who was responsible for cleaning the hands of the Temple Priest.

Plant Century

Represents immortality and everlasting life.

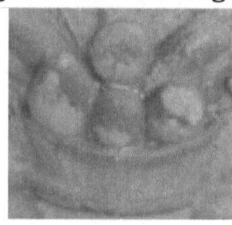

Plant Apple

Apples are one of the oldest and holiest symbols of life and rebirth among the Germanic folk, appearing as grave-gifts from the Bronze Age onward. Apples also represent salvation or sometimes sin.

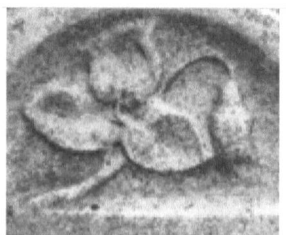

Plant, Broken Bud or Branch

Someone who died an untimely or premature death, usually seen on a younger person's gravestone.

Plant Calla Lily

A flower that represents beauty, a symbol reminiscent of the Victorian era, the Calla Lilly represents majestic beauty and is often used to represent marriage or resurrection.

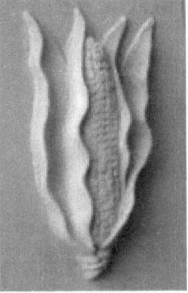

Plant Corn

Rebirth, fertility. It was a custom to send a bundle to relatives on the death of a farmer. It may be used as an occupational symbol.

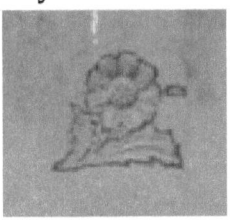

Plant Daisy

Symbolizes innocence; usually found on graves of young children.

Plant Dogwood

In Christianity, divine sacrifice, the triumph of eternal life, resurrection.

Plant, Fallen Tree

Mortality, death, a life cut short.

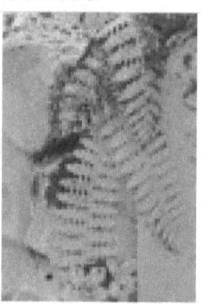

Plant Fern

Humility, sorrow, and sincerity.

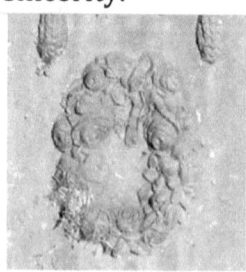

Plant Garland

Festoon or Garland. Maybe a garland of leaves, fruit, flowers, ribbon or fabric draped between two points. Originated from

Greek and Roman motifs, it symbolizes victory in death.

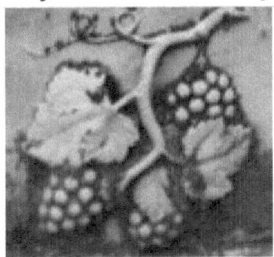

Plant Grapes
Blood of Christ. The grapevine is a symbol can be traced back to the ancient Greeks and is still used today as a symbol of fertility and prosperity.

Plant Ivy
Ivy carved into a tombstone is said to represent friendship, fidelity, and immortality.

Plant Laurel
Laurel, specially fashioned in the shape of a wreath, is a universal symbol found in the cemetery. It can represent victory, distinction, eternity or immortality.

Plant Lily

Symbol of virginity, purity, innocence - has been one of the symbols typically associated with the Virgin Mary. It was a popular funeral flower in Victorian times, symbolizing the returning of the soul to innocence at the time of death.

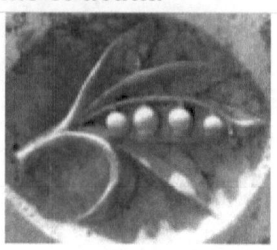

Plant Lily of the Valley

Purity, innocence, virginity - the return of happiness, virtue, humility.

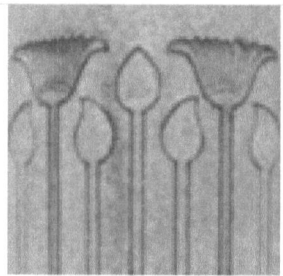

Plant Lotus

Commonly used in ancient Egypt and Hinduism, the flower is also sacred in Buddhism. It symbolizes the creation of life from the slime of the primordial waters. The closed lotus represents potential. With eight petals, it represents cosmic harmony; with 1,000 petals it means spiritual revelation.

Plant Morning Glory

Resurrection, mourning, youth, love, farewell, the brevity of life, departure, mortality.

Plant Oak Leaf
The mighty oak tree often represented as oak leaves and acorns signify strength, honor, longevity, and steadfastness. In Christain symbolism, it represents enduring faith. In the Native American culture, an oak leaf represents an Algonquian Tribe grave.

Plant Olive Branch
The olive branch, often depicted in the mouth of a dove, symbolizes peace - that the soul has departed in the peace of God. The association of the olive branch with wisdom and peace originates in Greek mythology where the goddess Athena gave an olive tree to the city that was to become Athens. An olive leaf also makes an appearance in the story of Noah. The olive tree is also known to represent longevity, fertility, maturity, fruitfulness, and prosperity.

Plant Palm Tree

Spiritual victory, success, eternal peace, a symbol of Christ's conquest of death as associated with Easter.

Plant Passion Flower

The elements of the passion of Christ: the lacy crown—the crown of thorns; the five stamens—the five wounds; the ten petals—the ten faithful Apostles.

Plant Pine Cone

Immortality from the evergreen tree - incorruptibility from the sap.

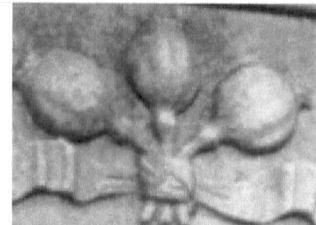

Plant Poppy

Poppies symbolize eternal sleep.

Plant Rose

Symbolizes beauty, a reminder that the soul achieves its most perfect state after physical death. A symbol of the blood of Christ also associated with the Virgin Mary, the 'rose without thorns.' A red rose symbolizes martyrdom, and a white rose symbolizes purity and virginity. Whether the rose is a bud, flower or somewhere in between indicates how old the person was at the time of death.

Plant Sunflower

Devotion to God and life fulfilled.

Plant Thistle

Thistles represent earthly sorrow. The thorns on a thistle symbolize the crown of thorns and the Passion of Christ. It is also found on many Scottish gravestones.

Plant, Tree or Trunk Stump

A tombstone in the shape of a tree trunk is symbolic of the brevity of life. Broken branches on the tree symbolize a life cut short.

Usually marks the graves of Woodmen of the World members. It is highly represented in cemeteries because, until the 1920s, one of the benefits of membership was a tombstone. Several organizations broke off from WOW including Women for Woodcraft, Neighbors of Woodcraft, Modern Woodmen of America, Woodmen Circle, and others.

Also, they usually contain other symbols such as anchors, lilies, vines, etc.

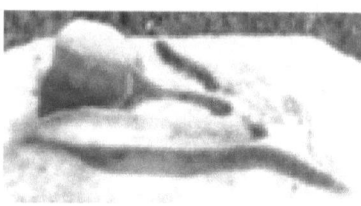

Plant Tulip

It symbolizes love and passion. As a flower, it is in rare bloom because it continues to grow after it is cut.

Plant Wheat

Time, the divine harvest at the end of life or life fulfilled. A sheaf of wheat represents yield, usually found on older peoples' gravestones.

Plant Willow Tree

Sadness or mourning. In the Native American culture, a willow tree represents an Iroquois Tribe grave.

Plant Wreath

Victory in death. The use of garlands, wreaths, and festoons dates back to ancient Greek times, and it was adopted into the Christian religion as a symbol of the victory of the redemption.

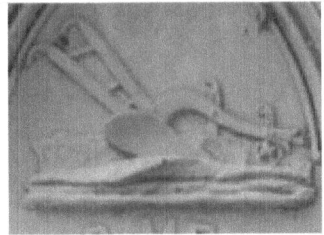

Plow

A plow symbolizes the harvest, the reaping of life.

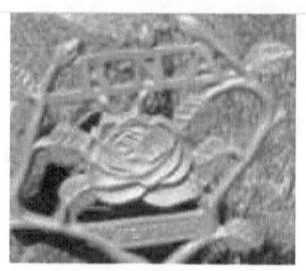

R.N.A.
Royal Neighbors of America, a non-profit fraternal membership organization that offers life insurance, annuities, and Medicare supplement for women. The first meeting was held in Council Bluffs, Iowa in January 1892.

Rabbit
Humility, gentleness, self-sacrifice.

Red Lettering
Chinese tombstones often appear before the decease of the commemorated. Red lettering shows that the person named is still alive. When that person dies, the stonecutter comes and repaints the letters in white.

Requiescit in Pace
Latin "rests in peace," also seen as initials R.I.P.

Ribbon, Red
An awareness ribbon colored red has several different meanings in different contexts. Foremost, it is the symbol of solidarity of people living with HIV/AIDS.

Rifle
Usually found on the graves of military members and hunters.

Rosary

Almost always found on Catholic gravestones, symbolizes devotion to Mary and constant prayer for the deceased person.

S.A.R.

Sons of the American Revolution, a fraternal society that was organized in 1889 for male descendants of American Revolutionary War veterans.

S.V.

Sons of Veterans of the United States of America, a group formed in 1881. They changed their name to the Sons of Union Veterans of the Civil War in 1925.

Saint Aldemar Commandery
A Knights Templar organization, Masonic.

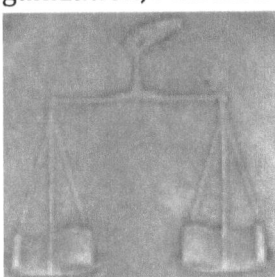

Scales
Often marks the grave of someone who was in the legal profession. Sometimes seen with a statue of Saint Michael, which symbolizes his duty of weighing the souls of the departed.

Scarab
An Egyptian symbol of spontaneous creation. Also symbolizes the renewal of life. When shown with falcon's wings it represents transcendence and protection.

Scroll

It symbolizes the scriptures, a symbol of life and time. Both ends rolled up to indicate a life that is unfolding like a scroll of uncertain length and the past and future hidden. Often held by a hand, representing life being recorded by angels.

Serpent, Brazen

Cross with a snake wrapped in it. The Brazen Masonic serpent is a symbol of the 25th Degree Masons. Christians also see this as foreshadowing Christ's salvific death upon the Cross.

Serpents, Caduceus

Staff entwined by two snakes. A caduceus, which is a short herald's staff entwined by two snakes (serpents) in the form of a double helix. Symbolizes someone who worked in the medical profession.

Seventh Day Adventist Church
Available emblem of belief for placement on government headstones and markers.

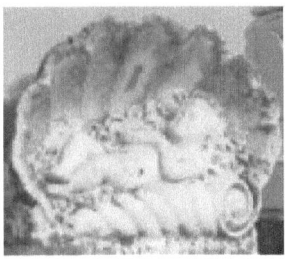

Shell
Baptism or rebirth. The use of shell in burials is pre-Christian in practice and pre-dates even Egyptian burial practices. Shell is symbolic of fertility, resurrection, and pilgrimage. Shells, coins, and small stones are the traditional objects left at grave sites.

Ship or Boat
Ships are usually found on the graves of sailors. Many times they are seen on graves of people who died at sea. They sometimes symbolize Noah's Ark, the ship that weathered the storm against all overwhelming odds.

Shoes

Empty shoes symbolize the loss of a child. Usually, one shoe is overturned.

Sickle

Death as the "last harvest."

Skull

Death and mortality. A winged skull symbolizes the ascension into heaven.

Skull and Crossbones

Mortality, Death.

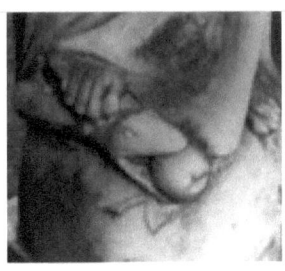

Snake with Apple
Sin, Satan, fall of man.

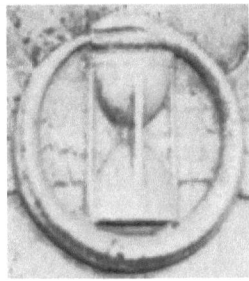

Snake, hooped
Symbolizes eternal life - no beginning, no end.

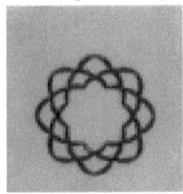

Soka Gakkai
Available emblem of belief for placement on government headstones and markers. Soka Gakkai is a Japanese Buddhist religious movement based on the teachings of the 13th-century Japanese priest Nichiren as taught by its first three presidents.

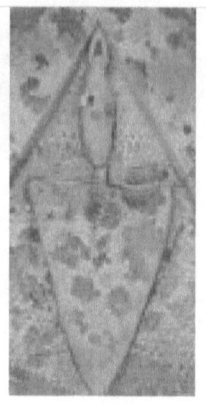

Spade

Symbolizes mortality and death, also used as a Masonic symbol.

Sphere

Ball or sphere usually a symbol of the soul waiting for resurrection.

Sphinx

The Sphinx, featuring the head and torso of a human grafted to the body of a lion, guards the tomb. It represents strength and protection. The male Egyptian sphinx is modeled after the Great Sphinx at Giza. The female, often appearing bare-breasted, is the Greek Sphinx.

Square and Compass

Usually, have the letter "G" in the middle. The square and compass represent the transition from the material to the intellectual to the spiritual. Found on gravestones belonging to members of the Freemasons (Masons).

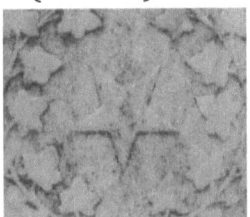

Star

Stars are ubiquitous for different faiths and military markers. A five-pointed star represents the Star of Bethlehem or Pagan or Muslim. A six-pointed star represents Creation or Jewish. Stars are also seen with the moon, sun, ivy or other combinations.

Star of David

Six-pointed star or Star of David, also known as Magen David (Hebrew for shield of David), it is typically used as a symbol of

Judaism. The star is actually made of two triangles. It signifies divine protection as epitomized by the alchemistic signs for fire and water which are an upward and downward apexed triangle.

Star, Cross and Shepherd's Crook

Symbol of the White Shrine of Jerusalem. Often seen with the phrase "In Hoc Signo Spes Mea," which translates to "In this Sign is my hope." A society for women who are related to (through birth, marriage, or legal adoption) to a Master Mason in good standing. Founded in 1894.

Star, Medal of Honor

The Medal of Honor is the highest military decoration awarded by the United States government. Available emblem of belief for placement on government headstones and markers.

Star, Nine Pointed

Symbol of the Baha'i Faith, a monotheistic religion. Available emblem of belief for placement on government headstones and markers.

Sun

A sun symbolizes the soul was rising to heaven. Sun is setting for death. Sun is rising for renewed life.

Sunburst with star and cross

Symbol of the First Corps of Cadets, now the 211th Military Police Battalion. "Monstrat Viam" is Latin for "It Points the Way."

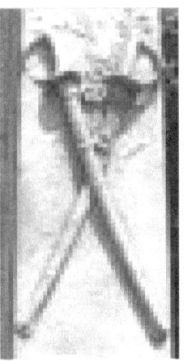

Sword

Swords represent martyrdom. Crossed swords are often seen on the gravestones of veterans, especially officers.

Sword, Crescent and Sphinx

Symbol of the Shriners (The Imperial Council of the Ancient Arabic Order of the Nobles of the Mystic Shrine). The group was founded in 1872 and can be joined once the member has become a Master Mason.

T.O.T.E.

Symbol of the Improved Order of Red Men, a patriotic society. TOTE means Totem of the Eagle.

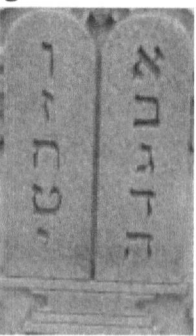

Tablets

Usually, two tablets joined, symbolizes the Ten Commandments, God's laws.

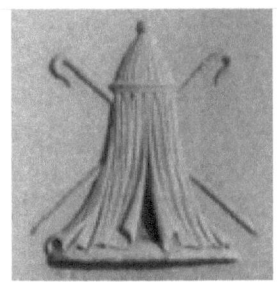

Tent

A symbol used by the Independent Order of Odd Fellows. The tent symbolizes their encampments, which are the three highest degrees attainable before reaching the most upper branch.

Tent, Dog

A small cemetery in Iowa, Captain William W. Ellis, a member of the 8th Pennsylvania and 61st Pennsylvania Infantry Regiments, is buried here.

Theatre Masks

Symbol of drama and theatre, also known as Comedy and Tragedy Masks.

Thor's Hammer

Available emblem of belief for placement on government headstones and markers. Thor is worshipped among other gods by Heathens, the followers of Ásatrú and Odinism. This approval happened in 2013, two headstones have been approved for it and is on my list to see.

Torch or Flame

Eternity. An upside down torch represents the end of life. A lit torch represents life, immortality and the everlasting life. Conversely, an inverted torch represents death or the passing of the soul into the next life. Generally, the inverted torch will still bear a flame, but even without the fire it still represents a life extinguished.

Tortoise

Tortoises or land turtles are land-dwelling reptiles. Like their marine cousins, the sea turtles, tortoises are shielded from predators by a shell. In Chinese culture, the tortoise is the symbol of heaven and earth, its shell compared to the vaulted heaven and the underside to the flat disc of the earth. It also stands for immutability and steadfastness.

Triangle with a star in the center

Symbol of the Order of the Sons of Temperance, a fraternal organization that promoted the temperance movement (abstinence and prohibition of alcohol). Usually seen with their motto: Love, Purity, Fidelity.

Triangle with square, spade, and keys

Symbolizes the York Rite of Masonry, the York Rite (sometimes referred to as the American Rite) is one of several Rites of Freemasonry.

Triangle with three T's joined at base

Symbol of the Royal Arch Masons (RAM). Royal Arch Masonry

(also known as "Capitular Masonry") is the first part of the York Rite system of the Masonic degrees.

U.A.O.D.

United Order of Ancient Druids, a fraternal organization. The Ancient Order of Druids (AOD) is a fraternal organization founded in London, England in 1781 that still operates to this day. It is the earliest known English group to be found based upon the iconography of the ancient druids, who were priest-like figures in Iron Age Celtic paganism.

U.V.L.

Union Veterans League, an organization for Union Civil War veterans. The Union Veterans was formed in Washington, D.C. in 1886 to fill a need of many Civil War Veterans.

Unitarian Church, Unitarian Universalist

Available emblem of belief for placement on government headstones and markers. Unitarian Universalism (UU) is a liberal religion characterized by no creed but instead are unified by their shared search for spiritual growth. As such, their congregations include many atheists, agnostics, and theists within their membership.

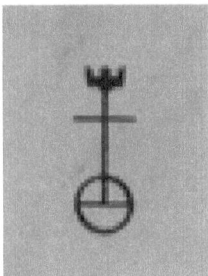

United Church of Christ

Available emblem of belief for placement on government headstones and markers. The United Church of Christ (UCC) is a mainline Protestant Christian denomination based in the United States.

United Church of Religious Science

Available emblem of belief for placement on government headstones and markers. The term "Science of Mind" applies to the teachings, while the term "Religious Science" applies to the organizations. However, adherents often use the words interchangeably.

Urn

The design represents a funeral urn and is thought to symbolize immortality. Classical symbol of death, particularly prevalent in the nineteenth century. The pot is commonly believed to testify to the end of the body and the dust into which the dead body will change, while the spirit of the departed eternally rests with God.

The cloth draping the urn symbolically guards the ashes. Flame on top of the jar the soul is departing, eternal vigilance, remembrance.

Veteran of the Cross
A veteran member of the Methodist Church.

W.B.A.

Woman's Benefit Association, a club for women that provided life insurance. Part of the Order of the Maccabees.

W.R.C.

Women's Relief Corp. It is the female auxiliary for the Grand Army of the Republic.

Wheel

The wheel represents the cycle of life, enlightenment, and divine power. Specific types of wheel symbols that might be found in the cemetery include the eight-spoked Buddhist wheel of righteousness, and the circular eight-spoked wheel of the Church of World Messianity, with alternating fat and thin spokes. A wheel might also represent a wheelwright.

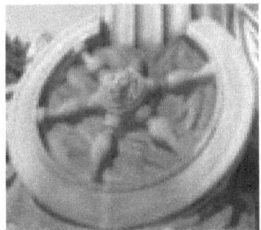

Wheel Broken

Symbolizes the end of life, a break in the circle or wheel of life.

Wheel of Dharma

The dharmachakra (which is also known as the wheel of dharma) is one of the Ashtamangala of Indian religions such as Jainism, Buddhism, and Hinduism. Available emblem of belief for placement on government headstones and markers.

Wicca

After a ten year legal battle, the circled pentagram (referred to as a pentacle) was added to the list of approved religious symbols to be placed on the tombstones of fallen service members in 2007. The decision was made following ten applications from families of fallen soldiers who practiced Wicca. Available emblem of belief for placement on government headstones and markers.

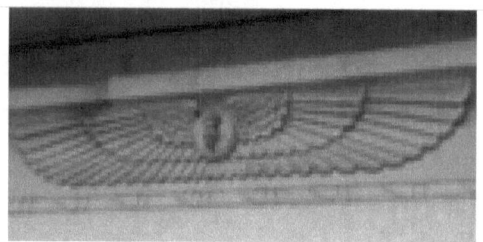

Winged Solar Disk

It is an ancient Egyptian symbol which represents the journey of the sun. Ra was the creator of the world, ancestor of the pharaohs and god of the sun (symbolized by the solar disk) and skies (symbolized by the wings). This is also a Zoroastrian symbol signifying many things.

Woman Clinging to Cross

Sometimes found with the verse "Rock of Ages cleft for me" or "Simply to the cross I cling." Symbolizes faith - a person or soul who is lost in the sea of sin, whose only hope is to cling to Christ's cross (the Rock of Ages).

Woman Holding Anchor

Represents hope. Early Christians used the anchor as a disguised cross, and as a marker to guide the way to secret meeting places.

Woman Holding Cross
Represents faith. The crucifix or cross can generate many symbolic messages ranging from love, faith and goodness to terror and fear.

Woman Weeping
Grief, or mourning an untimely death.

Woodmen Circle (W.C.)
Ladies auxiliary to the Woodmen of the World (WOW) members, an insurance company and fraternal organization. It is highly represented in cemeteries because, until the 1920s, one of the benefits of membership was a tombstone. Several organizations broke off from WOW including Women for Woodcraft, Neighbors of Woodcraft, Modern Woodmen of America, Woodmen Circle, and others.

Woodmen of the World

Seen on the gravestones of Woodmen of the World (WOW) members, an insurance company, and fraternal organization. It is highly represented in cemeteries because, until the 1920s, one of the benefits of membership was a tombstone. Several organizations broke off from WOW including Women for Woodcraft, Neighbors of Woodcraft, Modern Woodmen of America, Woodmen Circle, and others.

X.P.

The Chi-Rho, one of the oldest Christian symbols. XP is the first two letters of the Greek word for Christ.

Now see that was not so scary, right? Death is natural and is the only guarantee we have. Cemeteries tell us about the ethnic background of people, their occupations, how long they lived and, sometimes, what caused their deaths. They provide us with insights into cultural practices and beliefs. Some monuments are simple - a slab of wood or a carved piece of concrete with a name and dates scratched in. Others are elaborate sculptures.

What do you want your grave to say? Hopefully, this book has helped get a few ideas flowing. Cemeteries are a nonrenewable resource. Their survival is continuously threatened by expanding urban areas, vandalism, removal of headstones, theft of objects such as benches, gates and statuary, neglect and lack of fences to keep cattle from toppling headstones. If not cared for, these reminders of loved ones could be lost forever.

If you are planning your service (and you should), ask many questions. Often funeral directors only provide a few options to help ease the process. But there are many options they regularly don't inform you of or even know of.

If you are looking for historical data, keep searching. Cemeteries are like open history books whose pages are tablets of stone. Historians often consult cemetery records to confirm past events. Sometimes there is no other recorded information about an area except what can be found in cemeteries. Each one provides clues about the people who settled an area

If you picked the book for general use, keep reading. There is a lot of information out there that just does not fit into a single book or website.

Be respectful and go ahead, open the gate and walk in!

BIBLIOGRAPHY

Association for Gravestone Studies in Massachusetts.

"Available Emblems of Belief for Placement on Government".
    N.p., n.d. Web. 2012.

"Cemetery". Wikipedia. N.d. Web. 2012.

"Cemetery Photos". Ghost to ghost. N.d. Web. 2012.

"Gravestone Symbolism". Grave Addiction. N.d. Web. 2012.

"How to search a cemetery". Genealogical Institute. Utah. 1974.

Keister, Douglas. *Stories in Stone: A Field Guide to Cemetery
    Symbolism and Iconography*. Salt Lake City: Gibbs Smith,
    2004. Print.

"New Orleans Cemeteries". Nola Cemeteries. N.d. Web. 2012.

"Photo Gallery of Cemetery Symbols and Icons". ThoughtCo. N.d.
    Web. 2017.

"Random Exploration". UMW Blogs. N.d. Web. 2012.

"Symbols Found on Gravestones." The Cemetery Club. N.d. Web.
    2012.

"Tomb and Mausoleum Descriptions". Grave Addiction. N.d. Web.
    2013.

"Unearthly Delights". Zelinsky, Wilbur. Oxford University Press.
    1976.

"What does Graveyard mean?". Definitions.net. N.d. Web. 2017.

Countless questions asked around numerous cemeteries
    answered by cemetery employees, volunteers and visitors.
    Thank You!